tomcats
forever

VF-114

STALLIONS

FIGHTING 302

VF1

FIGHTING FIFTY ONE

FIGHTING 114

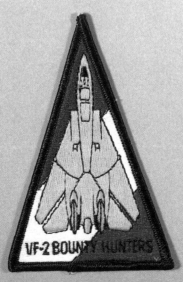

VF-2 BOUNTY HUNTERS

VF-211

tomcats
forever

David F Brown & Robert F Dorr

David F Brown is a law enforcement official in a township in Pennsylvania and an accomplished aviation photographer who travels extensively to catch warplanes in action at events like the Reconnaisance Air Meet and the London Ontario International Airshow. Brown's work has been seen in *Air Forces Monthly, Air International, Koku-fan,* and other journals. Dave obtained a degree in criminology from Indiana University of Pennsylvania and now resides in Thomasville with wife Christina and daughter Molly.

Robert F Dorr is a former diplomat and full-time writer, the author of *Phantoms Forever* in this series and other volumes on American military aviation. Dorr has a lifelong interest in air-to-air combat tactics and the development of fighter aircraft. Bob lives in Oakton, Virginia with his wife Young Soon and sons Bob and Jerry.

For the Tomcat Tweakers

Published in 1990 by Osprey Publishing Limited
59 Grosvenor Streeet, London W1X 9DA

British Library Cataloguing in Publication Data
Dorr, Robert F. 1939–
Tomcats forever.
1. Grumman F-14 aeroplanes, history
I. Title   II. Brown, David F.
623.74′64

ISBN 0–85045–967–2

Editor Tony Holmes
Designed by Paul Kime
Printed in Hong Kong

Front cover As a fighting machine, the Grumman F-14 Tomcat is only one cog in a much larger machine, the American military. No one is quite certain how all the cogs will fit together in an all-out war but the role of AWACS (airborne warning and control system) aircraft is certain to be important to everyone in the fight. Here, a VF-102 'Diamondback' occupies the same corner of sky as a Boeing E-3B Sentry AWACS aircraft [*Dave Parsons*]

Back cover Tomcats forever? Lieutenants Jack Fields and Mike Quillin of the 'Bounty Hunters' of VF-2 apparently think so as they bore through low-hanging murk along the American west coast in BULLET 203 on 15 June 1987. The fighter crew may be called upon to rise above the clinging gray stuff and vault into open space, but the Tomcat's pilot and radar intercept officer must also be prepared to deal with threats down low, where the gray and wet bombard the windshield like machine-gun bullets [*Dave Baranek*]

The design of the Tomcat appealed mightily to the Shah of Iran who became the only foreign customer for the F-14. Aircraft with bureau numbers 160299 to 160328 were supplied to Iran but the final machine in the series, 160328, was held up in the US after the Islamic revolution. See here in storage at David-Monthan AFB, Arizona, this 80th export Tomcat still wears Iranian camouflage. Since this photo was taken, 160328 was impressed by the US Navy and is now serving at Point Mugu [the Authors]

Introduction

America needs the F-14. That was the message appearing on American TV screens in the autumn of 1989 as the authors assembled this pictorial celebration of the US Navy's 'Top Gun' fighter. The F-14 had been in production for two decades, had served with one foreign user in addition to our navy, and although accruing some age, was still one of the best air-to-air combat machines this side of the long-awaited ATF (advanced tactical fighter). Many were concerned that production of the F-14 might end prematurely, and the TV message was intended to save not only the Tomcat but its builder, Grumman.

Other volumes may address the political, economic and corporate issues which underly the decision to end production early in the F-14D factory run. We are here not speak of politics but to show the Tomcat to our audience through the medium of photos. Photos aboard the carrier, photos returning from combat off the Libyan coast, and still more photos. None of these colour plates has ever been published before.

This work brings together words from one contributor, photos by the other, and additional illustrations from other fine photographers, whose names appear in the credits. It would not have been possible to create this appreciation of the Tomcat without Mike Anselmo, George Cockle, Joe Handelman, Tom Kaminski, Robert L Lawson, Don Linn, Barry Roop, and the others whose photos appear here. We are grateful to Dennis Baldry, Tony Holmes and Cathy Lowne who helped to make it happen. We dedicate this work to the Tomcat Tweakers, that stalwart breed of mechanics, electricians, radar experts, maintenance crews and deck crewmen who 'keep 'em flying' throughout the Fleet.

So enjoy. Enjoy the colour portraits that follow, a new way of looking at the Tomcat so far. The rest of the story will probably continue into the next century.

David F Brown
Thomasville, Pennsylvania

Robert F Dorr
Oakton, Virginia

The final checks are completed before a suitably marked VF-2 F-14 is taken aloft by a seasoned 'Bounty Hunters' crew from Miramar in August 1988. As is usual squadron practise, aircraft '201' is allotted to the unit commander, in this case BULLET 1 Commander Rip Serhan. On cruise this aircraft would occasionally be flown by no less a sailor than the skipper of USS *Ranger* (CV-61) himself. Befitting such a distinguished crew, this F-14, like the Commander Air Group's (CAG) '200', is maintained in pristine condition [*Tony Holmes*]

Contents

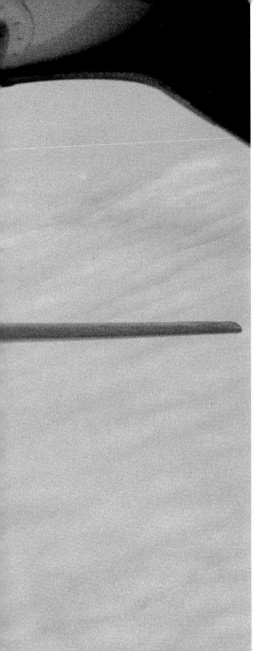

On the Boat

Left Grumman F-14A Tomcat 159010 coded AC-100 of the 'Red Rippers' of VF-11 links up on a McDonnell Douglas KC-10 Extender tanker on 13 June 1983, intent on sopping up some fuel with its probe and drogue air-to-air refuelling system. Refuelling has become integral to air combat operations and is now so routine that it is almost taken for granted − but even without it, the Tomcat has relatively long legs and can engage oncoming enemy aircraft far from its carrier battle groups [*via Authors*]

Above 'Felix the Cat' is the symbol of the 'Tomcatters' of VF-31. Even in these days of low-visibility markings, the squadron has always kept its CAG bird in what can only be called high visibility colours. BANDWAGON 200 may or may not be piloted by Commander Jesse Beaty, but the RIO's name is obscured in feline lore. Although both squadron and carrier belong to the Atlantic Fleet, *Forrestal* made a Vietnam cruise and VF-31, still flying F-4J Phantoms then, shot down a MiG-21 on 21 June 1972. Commander Samuel C (Sam) Flynn Jr. and Lieutenant William H (Bill) John were the MiG-killing crew. The 'Tomcatters' acquired their nickname long before the F-14 did and are the second oldest fighter squadron in the US Navy [*Jean-Francois Lipka*]

Full afterburner. Night is coming and night is the nemesis of the naval aviator. Nothing can affect an individual as strongly as flying off and returning to a carrier deck in the hours of darkness. Here, a 'Swordsmen' of VF-32 launches from USS *John F Kennedy* (CV-67) while the requisite Grumman A-6 Intruder waits patiently in the background [*via David F Brown*]

Opposite and bottom left On 14 September 1976 while President Ford was concluding the American bicentennial celebration, Tomcat 159588, coded AB-221 of the 'Swordsmen' of VF-32 rolled off the carrier's deck and went plunging into the North Sea off Scotland, complete with Phoenix missiles. Tomcat and Phoenix were new, and would have been of considerable value to the bad guys, so a complex and expensive operation was mounted to retrieve them from the bottom of the sea. The wrecked F-14A was eventually wrapped in a net and brought up, a permanent loss but at least one which did not fall into the wrong hands [USN]

Above AE-201 on USS *America* (CV-66) wears a low-visibility version of the VF-33 'Tarsiers' paint scheme. Though the design and appearance of aircraft carriers has changed dramatically over the years, the material used to coat the carrier deck has been unchanged since the last wooden-deck carrier, USS *Shangri-la* (CV-38) was retired in the early 1970s [*William Reigart*]

Above The distinction of 'blooding' the F-14 in combat fell to the 'Black Aces' of VF-41, a pair of squadron aircraft knocking down two Libyan Sukhoi Su-22M-2 *Fitter Js* over the Gulf of Sidra on 19 August 1981. Although this view of the aircraft with high-visibility markings apparently pre-dates the August 1981 shootdown by about three years, it is noteworthy that the Tomcat carries both Sidewinders and Sparrows and has blackening around its 20-mm cannon port from carbon deposits. Black radome is also unusual [*Angelo Romano*]

Right On the boat. It is interesting to ponder why FAST EAGLE 104 has such toned-down markings if its two crewmen are going into action wearing helmets as bright as a fire engine. In fact, the US Navy has adopted toned-down helmets since this view of a VF-41 'Black Aces' bird aboard USS *Nimitz* in 1982 was taken. The Tomcat was designed to accommodate its two-man crew without the need for a ladder, which would be awkward and unpopular on a busy carrier flight deck [*David F Brown*]

Left An impressive line-up of carrier aircraft on the nuclear-powered USS *Nimitz* (CVN-68), with a pair of VF-41 'Black Aces' Tomcats on the aircraft elevator in the foreground. The Vought RF-8G Crusaders in the immediate background are now history, with no more examples flying from American carriers. Other types are representative of current naval aviation, including the Grumman EA-6B Prowler which does an excellent job of screwing up the other guy's communications [*USN*]

Above Surrounded by red-shirted squadron armourers, a suitably drab VF-41 F-14A is soon to be armed-up with four AIM-7F Sparrow missiles which, for the time being, are firmly strapped to a small trolley beneath the starboard wing. Part of Air Wing 8 deployed on board the brand new USS *Theodore Roosevelt* (CVN-71), VF-41 was taking part in *Exercise Phinia '89*, a joint exercise involving both the US and French Navys. F-14s are usually armed and fuelled up on the carrier's stern, an area which could be termed 'Fighter Country' for the duration of the cruise [*Jean-Pierre Montbazet*]

For many years, the A-6 Intruder was Grumman's bread and butter, until questionable 1988 decisions resulted in cancellation of the A-6F and A-6G programmes. Destined for a continuing career well into the next century is the KA-6D Intruder, here exemplified by aircraft 155686 of the 'Black Falcons' of VA-85. The toned-down Tomcats gulping up fuel here belong to the 'Be-Devilers' of VF-74 and the 'Sluggers' of VF-103 [*USN*]

Currently partnering VF-41 aboard USS *Theodore Roosevelt* (CVN-71) is long-term sister squadron VF-84 *'Jolly Rogers'*, a unit which is perhaps the best known of all Tomcat operators. Wearing the colours which have attributed so much to the squadron's fame, the CAG-bird of VF-84 is connected up to the 'hopper' starter in preparation for spool-up. This beautifully decorated machine proudly wears a Battle 'E' on its fin, a symbol which denotes that the 'Reapers' have achieved a high level of combat readiness, and have maintained that level for a set period of time [*Jean-Pierre Montbazet*]

Right Could the launch crew be sharing a joke about the paint shop at VF-101? An extremely blotchy 'Grim Reaper' F-14A lines up behind a fellow squadron aircraft during carrier-quals on USS *America* (CV-66) in May 1988 [*Don Linn*]

Above In stark contrast to the CAG aircraft, this recently recovered F-14 is certainly more respresentative of VF-84's Tomcats. With the hook still firmly gripping the arrestor wire, and the crew still in the braced landing position, this F-14 will soon roll back slightly, disengage from the wire and taxy away towards the bow to allow other aircraft to recover. The marked two-tone low-viz scheme on the aircraft's nose is rather unusual [*Jean-Pierre Montbazet*]

Looking a little less shabby than its squadron mates, GRIM REAPER 163 is secured firmly to the catapult launch shuttle on board the *America*. The 'Reapers' hit the boat for a solid two weeks of fully-blown carrier aviation near the end of the trainee pilot's six-month course, this final test clinically separating true naval aviators from pretenders to the title. The intensity of the flying during the 14 days aboard ship is truly incredible, the aircraft only shutting down for refuelling. The lack of stores beneath this F-14 typifies the configuration of VF-101 aircraft during their time at sea [*Don Linn*]

Inset As the plane-guard SH-3H Sea King hovers alongside, an F-14 from the 'Fighting Diamondbacks' of VF-102 embarked aboard USS *America* (CV-66) prepares to launch from waist cat three. After the Tomcat is correctly fitted to the bridle, and the catapult is properly set for the aeroplanes weight, the launch crewman gives the traditional thumbs-up and the F-14 crew brace themselves for a gigantic kick in the behind [*Bill Reigart*]

F-14A Tomcat of the 'Fighting Diamondbacks' of VF-102 carrying an MSR (Mobile Sea Range) pod, a competing firm's version of the more widely used TACCTS (tactical air crew combat training system) pod. In ACM (air combat manoeuvring) and other forms of realistic training, the MSR and TACCTS pods receive inputs during simulated combat and help scorekeepers to later decide who won the 'war' [*Dave Parsons*]

Above 'Look, Ma!' On an earlier Mediterranean cruise, as indicated from the higher visibility of the band around their Tomcat, these 'Diamondbacks' have doffed their helmets and oxygen masks. It looks great for the folks back home, but we purists would probably prefer the crew of AB-211 to be seen in regulation flying gear. The aircraft carries live AIM-9 Sidewinder heat-seeking missiles [*Dave Parsons*]

Left Although Navy fighters usually draw fuel from Navy tankers, the F-14 Tomcat's probe and drogue refuelling system can be made compatible with the KC-135 Stratotanker or KC-10 Extender. Inclusion of air-to-air refuelling capability was essential to the fighter's design. Here, a 'Diamondback' of VF-102 refuels from KC-135 56-3610 [*Dave Baranek*]

Right When you are cruising in the sensitive waters of the South China Sea there is no room for dummy rounds on the wing and fuselage hardpoints, as this VF-1 'Wolfpack' F-14A clearly shows. Captured moments before launch from bow-cat one on board USS *Ranger* (CV-61) in April 1987, this VF-1 machine is armed with a single AIM-9L Sidewinder beneath the starboard wing glove, an AIM-7F Sparrow beneath the port wing glove and an extremely effective AIM-54B Phoenix snuggled beneath the fuselage. With this mix all eventualities should be covered. The squadron's long love affair with high-visibility colours even extends to the crew's bonedomes [*Tony Holmes*]

Above VF-1's marking were toned down not long after it flew missions in the neighbourhood of Saigon, but bad guys continued to appear in the squadron's gunsights. Here, in the late 1970s, side number 106 offers a strong reminder to not one but two Tupolev Tu-16 *Badgers* that it's prudent to follow the rules when playing with Tomcats. In mid-1989, the US and Soviet Union signed a new agreement aimed at preventing unwanted hostilities during mid-air encounters like this one [*USN*]

Oops. Naval aviators train hard to do it right, but sometimes doing it right means responding in the proper way when an unanticipated emergency arises. After taking the barrier and being foamed-down by alert firefighting crews, VF-1 'Wolfpack' aircraft NE-107 becomes an object of attention for the hard-working deck crews who will have to attach the aircraft to a hoist and use the crane to get it out of the way [*USN*]

Cruising along high above the clouds, this VF-2 F-14A wears squadron markings that were only fleetingly seen on 'Bounty Hunter' aircraft in 1987. The tail markings are basically a low colour version of the squadron's official badge, VF-2 reverting to their more colourful blue rudders and yellow topped tails, and red, white and blue nose striping, in early 1988 [*Dave Baranak*]

Inset Is the 'deck-driver' resting in the cockpit perhaps dreaming of what *he* could do in an F-14? During a lull between flight ops on board *Ranger* the recently recovered Tomcats are hauled back to the stern for refuelling. Having just participated in the exhausting two-week long *Exercise Team Spirit '87* off Korea, VF-2 and *Ranger* wound down in late April during the carrier's return cruise to San Diego [*Tony Holmes*]

Left above Apparently just back from a successful mission, NK-104 of VF-21's 'Freelancers', otherwise known as aircraft 161609, is now at rest until needed again. A nose wheel tow extension protrudes from beneath the front of the Tomcat and the main gear is chocked [*Mike Anselmo*]

Left below Side number 210 belongs to F-14A Tomcat 161619 of the 'Freelancers' of VF-21, getting ready to be launched from USS Co*nstellation* (CV-64) in October 1987. Even these Tomcat markings are relatively prominent compared with some US Navy aircraft, and are reminiscent of the squadron's former F-4J Phantom II paint scheme. The real low-viz colours of the modern Navy are reflected by the Grumman EA-6B Prowler sulking in the background [*Mike Anselmo*]

Above Side number 201 is lifting off on 15 October 1987. The black anti-glare shielding around this F-14 Tomcat's canopy area is not seen in most squadrons. The 'Freelancers' have been attached to CVW-14 and USS *Constellation* (CV-64) ever since they transitioned onto the F-14 in 1984 [*Mike Anselmo*]

Inset As the 1990s arrived, the future of these two aircraft was in question. Grumman KA-6D Intruder 152619 (NG-514) of the 'Boomers' of VA-165 refuels a Grumman F-14 Tomcat in mid-air over the Pacific in June 1981. By 1991, production of both aircraft was expected to cease and the future of their manufacturer appeared cloudy [*Dave Baranek*]

VF-24 Tomcat in flight, carryng Sparrows and Sidewinders, with wings in fully-swept position. Just above the port stabilator is the badge of the squadron's parent air wing, CVW-9. During this particular WestPac cruise on board USS *Ranger* (CV-61) in 1984, the 'Fighting Renegades' worked up with HMS *Invincible* in the Arabian Sea, partaking in air combat training with Fleet Air Arm Sea Harriers. Currently, along with sister squadron VF-211, VF-24 is transitioning onto the F-14A + (Plus), thus giving these two squadrons the distinction of being the first units on the Pacific coast to receive the new Tomcats [*Dave Baranek*]

If the aircraft is upside-down, the picture is right side up (we think). Of course none of this matters except in relation to the ground: air combat manoeuvring can occur at any attitude. Dave Baranek's favourite view of his favourite fighter shows side number 214 of the 'Fighting Renegades' of VF-24 in inverted flight during an aerial duel [*Dave Baranek*]

Left As viewed looking back over the shoulder from an accelerating Tomcat, this is a catapult shot from USS *Ranger* (CV-61) in Pacific waters in April 1983. This Tomcat belongs to the 'Fighting Renegades' of VF-24 [*Dave Baranek*]

Above With variable sweep wings in the 'slow' or manoeuvering position and both afterburners afire, this Tomcat is a formidable enemy. This dramatic look at an F-14A in mid-manoeuver was taken during flying activity by VF-24 'Fighting Renegades' near NAS Miramar, California in November 1983 [*Dave Baranek*]

Overleaf Tomcat on the tanker. The combat 'legs' of the F-14 are already impressive and can be extended substantially via in-flight refuelling. And although the usual refueller is a Grumman KA-6D Intruder, just about anything from KC-135 to KC-10 will do the job. In wartime, everybody in the fighting business will be in stiff competition for the limited number of tankers available. In this July 1982 view, the fuel is coming from a Marine Corps Lockheed KC-130F Hercules [*Dave Baranek*]

Overleaf inset It's the night that causes some naval aviators to throw down their wings of gold and look for something else to do for a living. Night operations from a carrier are inherently dangerous and disconcerting and since they aren't taught in training, the new F-14 jock learns them only upon reaching his F-14 fleet readiness squadron. Aboard USS *Ranger* (CV-61) in the Pacific in November 1983, a VF-24 'Fighting Renegades' F-14A Tomcat gives off an eerie green glow from its formation and navigation lights and a plume of fire from the afterburners of its twin TF30 turbofan engines [*Dave Baranek*]

Inset The 'Fighting Renegades' visit Japan. F-14A Tomcat 159621 (NG-204) aboard USS *Ranger* (CV-61) is seen during a stopover at Yokosuka in about October 1977. The port city has long been home to USS *Midway* (CV-41) which is not large enough to handle Tomcats but the visit by *Ranger* is somewhat unusual. Squadron VF-24 was still wearing colourful markings at this time [*via Robert F Dorr*]

In June 1981, F-14A Tomcat NG-206 of VF-24 is on afterburner as he climbs away from the clouds. In addition to under-fuselage fuel tanks, this Tomcat is carrying live AIM-7 Sparrow radar guided missiles rather than the blue-trimmed inert Sparrows often carried on routine peacetime missions [*Dave Baranek*]

Above The stationary 'frog' seems to be tailor-made for fitting beneath the instrument probe of this VF-51 'Screaming Eagles' F-14A. Photographed during Air Wing 15's WestPac cruise on board USS *Carl Vinson* (CVN-70) in 1986/87, the Tomcats of VF-51 during this time reflected what was probably the worst period for squadron colours ever. During the cruise the 'Screaming Eagles' not only operated in the scorching heat of the Persian Gulf, but also endured the freezing cold of the Bering Sea during winter, the flight deck often icing up while operations were underway [*Tony Holmes*]

Right These markings on a VF-51 'Screaming Eagles' F-14A Tomcat, with their dramatic eagle motif on the tail, were used for only one cruise and subsequently changed. NL-106 is heading for the steam catapult to be hurled into the air. The squadron was aboard USS *Kitty Hawk* (CV-63) in late 1979 when the carrier was rushed to the Persian Gulf as Americans were taken hostage in Tehran. More recently, VF-51 has operated from the deck of the nuclear-powered USS *Carl Vinson* (CVN-70) [*Bruce Sagnor*]

Above Another variation of the high-visibility red warpaint of VF-111's 'Sundowners' is apparent on NL-201, winging over the Pacific with variable geometry wings in the swept-forward position. Several thousand feet below, a loose formation of A-7E Corsairs struggle to keep in touch with the high flying 'Sundowner' [*USN*]

Left 'Block 100' Grumman F-14A-100-GR Tomcat 160674, alias NL-204, is almost ready for action on the deck of USS *Kitty Hawk* (CV-63) and reveals just one of many paint schemes used by the 'Sundowners' of VF-111, who got the idea for their colours from their successes against the Japanese in World War 2. The F-14A pilot will need to sweep the Tomcat's wings forward if he wants to be launched from *Kitty Hawk*'s catapult. The date is 28 April 1979. On 27 June 1981, this aircraft crashed into the Indian Ocean while operating from *Kitty Hawk* and was lost [*Phillip Huston*]

Above left Aboard the nuclear-powered USS *Enterprise* (CVN-65), F-14A Tomcat NH-114 wears a low-visibility version of standard markings for the 'Aardvarks' of VF-114. The Aardvark, otherwise known as zoology's African anteater, also shows his profile on the vertical tail. Wings of the Tomcat are in the farthest swept-forward position and the effect of sweeping them is apparent on the paint [*Lionel Paul*]

Below left Because Tomcats can be nudged close together when their wings are in the maximum sweep position, the F-14 is the first shipboard warplane since the Douglas A-4 Skyhawk to be built without folding wings. Side number 101 of VF-154 'Black Knights' aboard USS *Constellation* (CV-64) is receiving considerable attention from the deck crew prior to launch [*Mike Anselmo*]

Above Is he taking off or landing? For clues, note the absence of a tailhook and the afterburner fires erupting from the exhaust cans. F-14A Tomcat 161598, coded NK-111, of the 'Black Knights' of VF-154 is going aloft from USS *Constellation* (CV-64) in Pacific waters on 10 October 1987. The preservation of a little colour in VF-154's markings this late in the game is a sure sign that someone in the squadron has a sense of history, and it may even offer a glimmer of hope that in the 1990s things will improve [*Mike Anselmo*]

Miramar

Right No awards for guessing the owners of this F-14A. Bathed in the warm afternoon sun on the vast Miramar ramp, leader of the 'Wolfpack', Tomcat '100', is a beauty to behold in full VF-1 markings. Photographed between cruises in August 1988, 'Wolfpack' call Hangar One home when ashore. This hangar is also home to the legendary Naval Fighter Weapons School, VF-126 'Bandits' and the 'Bounty Hunters' of VF-2 [*Tony Holmes*]

Above As if trapped in a time warp, a stunning line-up of VF-1 tails prove that the low-viz message has not quite reached the 'Wolfpack' paint shop. First in line is Tomcat 162603, an F-14A-135-GR built in 1984. This particular airframe was in fact the sixteenth of 24 ordered in this block. As with the US Air Force, the Navy try and equip complete squadrons with aircraft from the same batch [*Tony Holmes*]

Perhaps the most beautiful markings ever worn by a Tomcat, even with a 'tourist' in the picture! These were the colours worn by the 'Wolfpack' of VF-1 when, together with the 'Bounty Hunters' of VF-2, they flew cover for the evacuation of Saigon on 30 April 1975. USS *Enterprise* (CVN-65) was one of several carriers in the region during *Operation Frequent Wind*, as the evacuation was named. Both squadrons are understood to have made flights over hostile Viet Cong and North Vietnamese forces, although it is thought that the F-14A Tomcat never made actual contact with the enemy [*via Authors*]

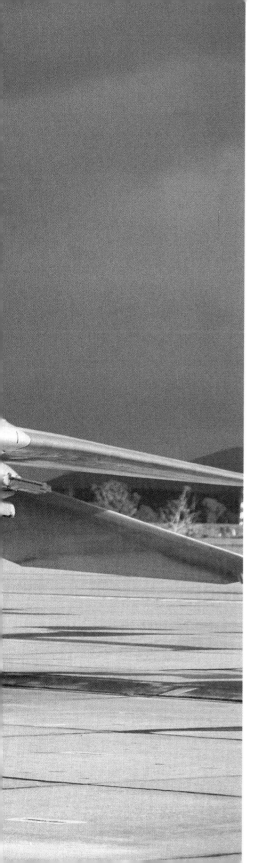

Left The TCS [Television Camera System] of this F-14A Tomcat is staring us in the face. VF-2 'Bounty Hunters' at NAS Miramar, California seem to have maintained their squadron markings through thick and thin. NL-210 had just come ashore from USS *Ranger* (CV-61) and was rendered even more colourful by the dark skies of a storm in the background. Friendly competitors in other squadrons refer to Fighting Two as the Avis squadron, based on the rental car company's one-time motto, 'We're number two so we try harder' [*Dave Baranek*]

Above In 1988 VF-2 scooped the pool in the annual Fightertown exercises, taking three of the four prizes up for grabs. The 'Bounty Hunters' won the Fighter Derby Trophy, the High Noon Gun Derby and the TARPS Exellence Trophy. As a result of these extensive work-up periods, VF-2 deployed with CVW-2 on board USS *Ranger* (CV-61) prepared for anything [*Tony Holmes*]

Inset Offering the best possible contrast between low and high visibility markings, this line-up of 'Bounty Hunters' was seen at Miramar in August 1988. At the time it was hard to tell whether the squadron was in the process of low-vizing their aircraft, or repainting them in traditional VF-2 colours. Tomcat 162604 is the sister F-14 to the VF-1 aircraft seen earlier heading up the 'Wolfpack' line [*Tony Holmes*]

It's not certain whether any Navy fighter squadron, even one as good as VF-24, is 'world renowned' — but the sign of the hangar says so. Grumman F-14 Tomcat 159617, coded NG-210, makes a pretty picture sitting at home base on 17 January 1976, an early date in the history of the famous fighter. 159617 crashed into the Pacific Ocean off San Clemente Island on 14 June 1982 and must now be included among those Tomcats which have been written off [Gerry Markgraf]

Right The paint scheme on US Navy warplanes was not designed to mask them against a backdrop of snow-covered mountains but it does have that effect. On 2 June 1981, a quintet of F-14A Tomcats from the 'Fighting Renegades' of VF-24 wings over the High Sierra en route to Miramar. Worldwide operations by the fourteen US carrier battle groups subject the F-14 Tomcat to operations in every extreme of climate, from the frozen north to the parched heat of the tropics [*Robert L Lawson*]

Above It wasn't intended for the purpose, but the low-viz paint on today's Tomcats can sometimes seem almost green and can fade into a background of fields and foliage. VF-24 'Fighting Renegades' Tomcat from Miramar, working out near El Centro, California, has no brightness anywhere and seems lost against its background. It will fool the bad guys, but isn't it sometimes a handicap to the good guys to be so difficult to spot? [*Dave Baranek*]

Both 160670 and 160672 have been lost in mishaps, but as this volume went to press Grumman F-14A Tomcat 160671 was still performing for the Navy. More than a decade ago, on 9 September 1978, coded as CAG BIRD NL-100 for the 'Screaming Eagles' of VF-51, this Tomcat had come ashore from USS *Kitty Hawk* (CV-63) and was posing in bright sunshine at NAS Miramar, California. In more recent times, it is a fair bet that 160671 is a little less colourful [*Phillip Huston*]

Above left At least a decade later, this 'Screaming Eagle' of VF-51 at NAS Atsugi, Japan has sunk to the very lowest of low-viz, so low, indeed, that the line chief probably has to scratch his head upon receiving an order to 'run down that row and fix up SCREAMING EAGLE 113.' Once more we see how difficult it must be for modellers to imitate real life given the various shades in today's drab Navy colours [*via Authors*]

Below left Rarely does an interesting aeroplane venture to this setting, replete with Rocky Mountain backdrop, without falling into Bob Greby's lens. At Petersen AFB in Colorado Springs, some distance away from the nearest aircraft carrier, we see a 'Sundowner' of VF-111, the squadron whose markings are based on the wartime Imperial Japanese Navy flag. 160676, coded NL-202, is from Air Wing 15 embarked aboard USS *Carl Vinson* (CVN-70) [*Robert B Greby*]

Above Back-seater Dave Baranek's notes on this picture say, 'August 1985: Two F-14s from each VF-51 and VF-111 return to Miramar from co-ordinated strike at China Lake Electronic Warfare Range, with three of the bogeys.' The closest Tomcat appears to be wearing the ficticious squadron insignia associated with the motion picture 'Top Gun'. The bad guys in this shot are Northrop F-5E and F-5F adversary aircraft. Three other Tomcats involved in this day's mission are not visible [*Dave Baranek*]

Inset It remains something of a mystery why the Navy and Air Force has not adopted the Ferris disruptive camouflage scheme. Both services tested this version of warpaint on F-4 Phantoms and it has subsequently been seen on F-14 Tomcats and F-15 Eagles – but never in squadron service. It seems clear that the paint job does what's intended – it confuses the bad guys visually. NJ-410 of VF-124 'Gunfighters' is F-14A Tomcat 159827, seen at NAS Miramar, California on 29 January 1978 [*Phillip Huston*]

'Aardvark' from an earlier, higher-visibility era. F-14A Tomcat 159852 coded NH-101 from VF-114 lifts away from NAS Willow Grove, Pennsylvania on 5 July 1978. This version of the squadron's paint scheme is identical to the one used earlier on 'Aardvark' F-4 Phantoms and is typical of the colourful designs found on many Navy aircraft in the 1970s. The nose wheel door of the Tomcat has not yet retracted. The blackening effect of carbon is evident around the housing for the nose 20-mm cannon [*Barry Roop*]

Inset 159463 of VF-124 in an early Tomcat view from about June 1975. The Tomcat is one of the few Navy aircraft which has a proper air conditioner capable of working on the ground as well as in the air, unlike Buckeyes, Skyhawks and other types which are best taxied with the canopy open. [*via Authors*]

This aircraft has quite a story behind it. Seen on the Miramar ramp in early August 1988, AARDVARK 100 was specially painted up in full VF-114 colours for several reasons. Firstly, and most importantly, the 'Aardvarks' had just been awarded the 1987/88 Joe Clifton Award for being the top fighter squadron in the whole US Navy. Secondly, VF-114 had also won the Battle 'E' and Safety 'S' awards from the Chief of Naval Operations for sustained combat readiness, maintained without accidents. And thirdly, the 'Aardvarks' had just seen a change of command ceremony and this aircraft was used as a backdrop for the function. Unfortunately only one side of the Tomcat was decorated, the port half remaining all grey. Soon after this photo was taken Tomcat 100 was wheeled into the paint shop and resprayed in tactical greys, just like the remaining 11 F-14As on strength with VF-114 [*Tony Holmes*]

Perhaps least-known among all Tomcat squadrons was the short-lived 'Satan's Kittens' of VF-191 which had exceedingly brief careers with both the F-4 Phantom II and the F-14 Tomcat. Aircraft 161298, numbered as NM-101 is taxying at Willow Grove, Pennsylvania on 14 October 1987. A Warminster, Pennsylvania Lockheed P-3 Orion is visible in the background. Note raised spoilers and back-seat radar intercept officer's partially deployed hood. VF-191's brief existence as a fighter squadron lasted a whole 18 months, the unit, along with sister Tomcatters VF-194 'Legendary Red Lightnings', being a victim of the severe 1988 fiscal budget which saw CVW-10 disestablished on 30 September 1988 [*John D Shields*]

Above left Viewed in the glare of a sun so bright that it could only be shining in Las Vegas, Gruman F-14A Tomcat 161146, alias NG-100 of the 'Fighting Checkmates' of VF-211 shows off its chequerboard style during a visit to Nellis AFB, Nevada on 20 August 1984. Navy fighters routinely visit Nellis to engage in mock aerial duels with the Air Force, and it is not impossible that a Tomcat may have come upon an F-117A Stealth fighter or two [*Keith Svendsen*]

Below left Not all squadrons have their CAG and CO mounts painted up in full colours, VF-211 'Checkmates' being one such unit. Getting a thorough scrubbing after flight ops at Miramar in August 1989, this Tomcat has had major surgery performed on its rear end. Now powered by new General Electric F110-GE-400 turbofans, this aircaft was part of 'Block' 125 built in 1982. For seven years the Tomcat served the fleet faithfully before returning to Grumman where it was transformed into an F-14A + (Plus). Besides the 29 new build aircraft produced to this uprated standard by Grumman, 40 older F-14As have been pulled from fleet squadrons and suitably modified [*Michael M Anselmo*]

Above Apparently this F-14A Tomcat belongs to VF-213 'Black Lions', but it has no tailcode and no side number, and a silhouetted map of Texas has been emblazoned on its tail, perhaps an act of chicanery by someone at NAS Dallas. The bureau number is 159869 [*Pete Wilson*]

Oceana

One squadron not heavily featured in this volume is VF-11 'World Famous Red Rippers'. Part of CVW-6, and attached to USS *Forrestal* (CV-59), the 'Rippers' have flown the F-14 since the summer of 1980. Seen here participating in a Red Flag exercise at Nellis in April 1987, the 'Rippers' aircraft wear battle efficiency and safety awards on their rudders. VF-11 has not suffered too much with the advent of low-viz colours because their markings were quite sedate to start with! One of the squadron's maintainers has loosened an engine panel and is busily inspecting the aircraft's port TF30. Originally powered by the -412A model Pratt & Whitney, all fleet F-14s were re-engined between February 1977 and June 1979 with the more powerful TF30-P-414 turbofan, an engine which mostly solved early powerplant difficulties [*Brian C Rogers*]

Right F-14A Tomcat 160400, coded AC-102, of the 'Red Rippers' of VF-11 at NAS Oceana, Virginia on 2 October 1982. The Oceana ramp, which once boomed to the sound of Phantoms' J79 engines, has been the east coast home of the TF30-powered Tomcat since the onset of the 1980s. As many as a hundred Tomcats may be seen on the flight line of this naval air station near Virginia Beach on a good day. Nearby is Norfolk, where Atlantic Fleet aircraft carriers are often moored [*Robert F Dorr*]

Above The men. The 'Tophatters' of VF-14, who were embarked aboard *John F Kennedy* (CV-67) together with VF-32 'Swordsman', come home from the Mediterranean and walk from their aeroplanes at NAS Oceana, Virginia on 31 January 1989. Side number 101 belongs to Tophatter One, CDR Pete (Strick) Strickland. The amount of talent assembled in this one picture almost defies the imagination. For every step each of these men took along the road to becoming a naval aviator, others were unable to qualify at the beginning or faltered along the way. As the film 'Top Gun' proclaimed, these men are the 'best of the best' [*David F Brown*]

A squadron with a very long history, VF-14 'Tophatters' have flown many
different types of naval aircraft, and performed many roles since they were
established in September 1919. Along with sister-squadron VF-32, the
'Tophatters' became the very first east coast F-14 unit when they transitioned
onto the Tomcat at Miramar in early 1973. Captured on film on the Oceana
ramp in April 1979, this CAG aircraft carries markings which are still
representative of the squadron over a decade later [*Jim Tunney*]

Side view illustrates landing gear design, sleek fuselage contours, and Sparrow missile wells. Another 2 October 1982 view at Oceana depicts 161149, coded AC-212, with VF-31's familiar 'Felix the Cat' emblem on the fuselage. A year later this same aircraft, still with the same markings and side number, developed problems on an 11 November 1983 flight over the Mediterranean near Lebanon. The crew ejected and this Tomcat plunged into the sea [*Robert F Dorr*]

Carrying a pair of underbelly tanks and a single AIM-7F Sparrow on the wing shoulder pylon, TOMCATTER 203 recovers at NAS Oceana after a long Atlantic cruise on board USS *Forrestal* (CV-59). The all-black nose is as much a symbol of VF-31 as the 'Felix the Cat' emblem, the squadron having darkened many a radome during their post-war existence [*David F Brown*]

Inset Through thick and thin VF-31 have managed to keep the twin fins of their Tomcats blood red. Having just been washed and left out to dry on the Oceana ramp, Tomcat 211 is every bit a proud VF-31 machine [*David F Brown*]

Inset An early (14 October 1977) view of F-14A Tomcat 159601, coded AB-223 belonging to the 'Swordsmen' of VF-32. After transferring to the 'Ghostriders' of VF-142 and inheriting modex AG-214, this Tomcat crashed into the sea while on approach to USS *Dwight D Eisenhower* (CVN-69) on 6 March 1980 [*Phillip Huston*]

Looking as pristine as a brand new Cadillac on a showroom floor, this early F-14A, BuNo 159008, belongs to the 'Swordsmen' of VF-32. Photographed just after the squadron had returned from transitioning onto the F-14 at Miramar, the CAG machine was found hiding in a hangar at Oceana in September 1974. The authors believe that this aircraft crashed near Oceana on 31 October 1977 while attached to VF-101 [David F Brown]

Right The well-known Tomcat leans against the bar, looks at the stranger in town who wants to pick a fight, and says, 'Anytime, baby'. For a brief period, the Tomcat character became a buccaneer on the tails of the 'Swordsmen' of VF-32, as on TARPS (tactical airborne reconnaissance pod system) equipped F-14A Tomcat 161158 (coded AE-211) on approach for a visit to Andrews AFB, Maryland on 13 May 1983 [*Barry Roop*]

Above AC-201 returns to the east coast home of the F-14, NAS Oceana, Virginia on 31 January 1989 after a Mediterranean cruise aboard USS *America* (CV-66). During the cruise, *America*'s Tomcats shot down two Libyan MiG-23 fighters in an impromptu air-to-air engagement. Although it is not one of the MiG-killing Tomcats, aircraft 162694 (coded AC-201) of the 'Swordsmen' of VF-32 has two tiny Libyan insignia (green flags) painted on its canopy rails behind the names of the crew [*David F Brown*]

Its tyres screeching, GYPSY 210 settles down at NAS Oceana, Virginia on 31 January 1989 following the cruise aboard USS *John F Kennedy* in which this squadron despatched two MiG-23s from Colonel Khaddafi's Al Bumbah airfield [*David F Brown*]

FAST EAGLE 107, alias Grumman F-14A Tomcat 160390, was one of two Tomcats which blew a pair of Libyan Sukhoi Su-22 *Fitters* out of the sky on 19 August 1981. The other machine, side number 102, was in the hands of Commander Hank Kleeman and Lt Dave Venlet. 107 was crewed by Lt Larry (Music) Mucsynski and Lt Jim Anderson. The engagement was begun when an Su-22 fired an *Atoll* missile at the pair of Tomcats. The Tomcat crews, belonging to the 'Black Aces' of VF-41, finished off the engagement with AIM-9L Sidewinder missiles, producing the much-publicized score of two to nothing [*via Authors*]

Inset Just back from the eventful 1988-89 *John F Kennedy* Mediterranean cruise GYPSY 213 basks at NAS Oceana, Virginia on 31 January 1989. During the 76-second engagement with the MiGs, VF-32 crews fired three AIM-7 Sparrows and one AIM-9 Sidewinder. Libya's air-sea rescue forces were unable to save the two pilots, who ejected and had 'good' chutes but were not recovered. A few days after the Oceana stopover, the squadron moved on to Roosevelt Roads for live missle-firing exercise with live Phoenixes [*David F Brown*]

Another 'Black Aces' F-14 Tomcat, this time aircraft 160388, taking off from NAS Oceana, Virginia on 13 October 1978. While still wearing side number 105 with VF-41, this Tomcat crashed in the sea on 1 April 1980 while flying from USS *Nimitz* (CVN-68). At the time, *Nimitz* was operating near the Persian Gulf in connection with efforts to secure the release of American embassy personnel being held hostage in Tehran [*Barry Roop*]

'Moon-equipped' is an inside joke based upon an American television commercial and appears on this VF-101 'Grim Reaper' because the pilot of the Tomcat is a Commander Moon. F-14A Tomcat 161134 (AD-101) of the replacement air group is a TARPS-equipped aircraft ready and able to take on the reconnaissance function. The location is NAS Oceana, Virginia on 30 April 1983 [*Joseph G Handelman, DDS*]

Flown no doubt by a seasoned crew from the 'Grim Reapers', a softly camouflaged F-14A recovers at Bergstrom AFB during RAM 88. Obviously a VF-101 machine, even the external tanks have 'Ripper' stencilling emblazoned upon them. The overall finish of the Tomcat's paint scheme suggests that VF-101 were making a big push for the Concours prize for the best presented aircraft at the RAM meet [*David F Brown*]

The man of the hour, the hero of our story, the guy to whom this volume is dedicated – the Tomcat Tweaker who fixes it, maintains it, helps to move it around on the deck, and keeps it flying. This maintenance crewman of US Navy Fighter Wing One (Fitwing One) was on the scene at RAM 88, the annual reconnaissance competition held at Bergstrom AFB, Texas, where TARPS-equipped Tomcats performed admirably. Pilots and radar intercept officers may come and go, but Tomcat Tweakers are a special breed, with the staying power the Navy needs to fight and win
[David F Brown]

Right Three-quarter rear view of an F-14A shows some of the key design features of the US Navy's first-line fighter. Tailhook is located between engine afterburner exhaust cans. Main landing gear doors can close while gear is down. Twin vertical tailfins help during 'energy' manoeuvering while the canopy covering crew members is a single long, glass cover. 161419, coded AD-173, belongs to VF-101 'Grim Reapers', and is seen at NAS Oceana, Virginia on 2 October 1982 [*Robert F Dorr*]

Above Once finished with flight training in T-34C Mentor, T-2C Buckeye and TA-4J Skyhawk, naval aviators lucky enough to qualify for the Tomcat go to a Fleet Replacement Squadron (FRS) which most of them still call a 'Rag' after the obsolete term Replacement Air Group (RAG). The east coast Tomcat training squadron is the 'Grim Reapers' of VF-101 whose symbol of death appears on the tail of 162688, seen at the 1988 London Ontario Airshow. The 'triple nuts' or triple zero side number indicates that the aircraft is set aside for a flag-rank officer, in this instance Rear Admiral Jimmie Taylor, who is Chief of Naval Air Training or CNATRA, inevitably pronounced Sinatra [*David F Brown*]

Above right The 'Grim Reapers' regularly perform up and down the east coast during the summer at a variety of airshows, waving the flag for naval aviation. On 1 June 1985 at the London Ontario Airshow, 161604 (AD-141) passed low over the crowds and into Barry Roop's lens. Even in the days when Navy markings were colourful, the paint scheme for the 'Reapers' was . . . well, grim, and this Tomcat does not disappoint! [*Barry Roop*]

Below right Grumman F-14A + (Plus) Tomcat with distinctive enlarged afterburner exhausts during routine operations at NAS Oceana, Virginia. The aircraft belongs to VF-101, the 'Grim Reapers' introducing the new Tomcat into front line squadron service in early 1988 [*David F Brown*]

Above Possibly an ex-VF-31 'Tomcatters' F-14A, this VF-101 machine has a non-standard black nose. Seen taxiing out at Oceana in July 1988, Tomcat 161860 was one of 30 aircraft ordered in the 'Block' 130 group delivered in 1983. The student pilot is checking the aircraft's wing spoilers during the long trip out to the runway [*David F Brown*]

A Tomcat flies formation on a wingman in 1988, preparing to land at Naval Air Station Oceana, Virginia. The Virginia farmland looks nice but the near-ultimate in lack of colour on Navy aircraft has finally been attained. DIAMONDBACK 104 will not be easy to spot by any hostile MiG pilot, but it also will not be easily distinguished from VF-102's other fighters on a pitching carrier deck, at night, in a rainstorm. With the de-emphasis on sharp, clear markings, nobody wants to be the mechanic who is told to, 'run down that line of parked aeroplanes until you get to 104 and get to work on her.' There have been instances of maintenance crews repairing the wrong aeroplane because of the lack of distinctive markings [*Dave Parsons*]

Left Wearing a curious blend of low-viz colours and fully blown squadron markings, a VF-102 Tomcat cruises over rugged terrain many miles from its lush green home of Oceana. The pilot has the aircraft's variable geometry wings fully swept forward, and the F-14 appears to be hanging in the sky just waiting to pounce on any unsuspecting prey that may be lurking miles below [*Dave Parsons*]

Above Very similar to the tail marking of the 'Grim Reapers' is the tail icon seen here for the 'Ghostriders' of VF-142. An Atlantic Coast fleet squadron, this aircraft was photographed at its home of Oceana on 2 May 1981. The aircraft is 159431, coded ND-200, the 'double nuts' or double zeros in the side number indicating that it is a CAG aircraft. The skipper of a Carrier Air Wing is known as CAG based upon the older term Carrier Air Group. The smoke in the background is not Tomcat-related [*Stephen H Miller*]

Above One fighter squadron not extensively featured in this volume is the east coast/Atlantic Fleet 'Sluggers' of VF-103, seen here during a visit to Pease AFB, New Hampshire on 28 May 1988. Markings seen here are similar to the squadron's markings during its F-4 Phantom era. SLUGGER 201 is devoid of missiles or droptanks and may be getting ready to fly out to USS *Independence* (CV-62) [*Barry Roop*]

Above right We think that's probably Rutherford and Sayers presiding over GHOSTRIDER 201, the callsign for Grumman F-14A Tomcat 162699, as the jet descends toward Oceana in a freeze-frame likeness that bears Dave Brown's trademark. The 'Ghostriders' of VF-142 were operating from USS *Dwight D Eisenhower* (CVN-69) and the other co-author promises to get Brown a date stamp with proceeds from this volume [*David F Brown*]

Below right If ever a prize was to be awarded to a squadron for the most tasteless unit motto, VF-143 would win hands down! Proudly titled the 'Pukin' Dogs', the squadron transitioned onto the F-14 from the venerable F-4J Phantom II in 1974. Along with a change in aircraft came a change in coasts, the former Miramar-based 'Dogs' being transferred to Virginia. Rather overshadowed by the remnants of Hurricane Clarence, VF-143 groundcrew perform an engine check on the CO's mount at Oceana in September 1988 [*Tony Holmes*]

Reserves, testers and prototypes

Grumman F-14A Tomcat 162708 (coded AF-104) of the Dallas-based Naval Air Reserve squadron, the 'Rangers' of VF-201, descends for a landing at its Texas home. 162708 is a new-build aircraft which went direct from the factory to the Reserves. Reserve units have the oldest and newest Tomcats in service. Note that the tailcode of the aircraft is surrounded by an outline of the Lone Star State [*Steve Tobey*]

Left Represented abroad USS *America* (CV-66) during Atlantic coast work-ups on 2 May 1989, the 'Superheats' were some distance from their Dallas home. When taxying on the crowded carrier deck, the F-14 keeps wings back at maximum sweep in order to make the aircraft as narrow as possible, but when being launched from the catapult the wings are swept forward for optimum low-speed and low-level flight conditions. Although this Tomcat is another classic case of Dullsville as far as colours are concerned, the squadron certainly regards the aircraft as a quantum leap ahead of the F-4 Phantom II it flew for many years. Reserve aircrews receive the same training and perform the same carrier operations as full-time Navy people but do not normally deploy on a carrier for an extended cruise [*Don Linn*]

Above The second Naval Air Reserve squadron which operates Tomcats from NAS Dallas, Texas, is nicknamed 'Superheats' and designated VF-202. Side number AF-204 is F-14A Tomcat 158629, seen over Dallas on 16 October 1987 [*Steve Tobey*]

Right Wearing small USS *Enterprise* titles on its supersonic glove vanes, this rather nondescript F-14A belongs to reserve squadron VF-301 'Devil's Disciples'. Although not regularly assigned to a fleet carrier, VF-301, and sister-squadron VF-302, deploy to sea with the rest of CVWR-30 once every two years for a brief period. The *Enterprise* titles were sprayed onto VF-301 aircraft in preparation for the unit's 12-day stay on the 'Big E' in August 1988. Rumour has it that, between them, VF-301 and 302 have 48 experienced pilots and RIOs on their books! This aircraft was seen at Miramar just prior to the 'Disciples' deployment in early August 1988 [*Tony Holmes*]

Above Visiting Westover AFB, Massachusetts on 5 March 1988, this Grumman fighter has been left alone at Hangar 5 amid late winter's snow and slush. F-14A Tomcat 158989, coded ND-200, of the 'Stallions' of Naval Air Reserve squadron VF-302 is a long way from its Pacific Fleet/west coast roosting at NAS Miramar near San Diego, where the weather is undoubtedly better [*Robert Rys*]

Left At RAM 88, the much-publicized Reconnaissance Air Meet held annually at Bergtrom AFB, Texas, TARPS-equipped ND-213 touches down. Pilots of aircraft intended for carrier operations must un-learn an otherwise wholly normal tendency to flare out at runway's end. Because a carrier aircraft may have to go around again, the pilot is instructed to make a very solid landing whilst ready and able to jam the throttles full forward. Even when operating from land, carrier pilots inevitably make carrier-style landings. Belonging to the 'Stallions' of VF-302, a Naval Air Reserve outfit, this reconnaissance Tomcat is in a particularly 'low' version of low visibility paint. Some observers believe that the era of toned-down markings and camouflage may have peaked and that we may see brighter and more colourful carrier aircraft in the 1990s [*David F Brown*]

Above F-14A + (Plus) Tomcat 162911 (coded XF-51) of VX-4 settles for a landing during a visit to Nellis AFB near Las Vegas on 16 March 1989. 162911 is one of the newest Tomcats off the production line and was built from the outset as an A Plus aircraft with larger afterburner units. The low-visibility grey paint scheme is far from satisfying to modellers but is typical of the US Navy in the 1980s and 1990s [*Barry Roop*]

Left Viewed from below is F-14A + (Plus) Tomcat 161444 making a slow roll over the London Ontario Airshow in 1989. The updated A Plus version of the Grumman fighter has larger afterburner cans and dispenses with the wing glove vanes found on the A model. This airframe went back to the manufacturer to be brought up to A Plus standard. At the onset of the 1990s, the arrival of lean budgets made it possible that production of the very last F-14 Tomcat could occur as early as March 1991. Even if production were curtailed, however – and many leaders in Washington did not want to see a curtailment – the Tomcat was surely likely to remain in service at least until the year 2010. So our 'celebration' of the Tomcat comes not at the conclusion of the story but in its middle [*David F Brown*]

Below Used with permission from Hugh Hefner's magazine, the *Playboy* bunny has adorned more than one aircraft belonging to the 'Evaluators' of VX-4 assigned to NAS Point Mugu, California. F-14A Tomcat 161444, coded XF-47, found itself surrounded by snow during a 2 January 1984 visit to Andrews AFB, Maryland. This machine is a 'Block' 120 aircraft, meaning that its full designation is F-14A-120-GR [*Eugene L Zorn*]

XF-47, otherwise known as F-14A Tomcat 161494 belongs to VX-4 at NAS Point Mugu, California, but is seen on a rare inland visit to Great Falls, Montana in May 1987 [*Jim Benson*]

Inset VX-4's 'Black Bunny', replete with un-black AIM-54B Phoenix missile, at an airshow, possibly at home at NAS Point Mugu, California. This paint scheme was worn for a long period by F-4J Phantom 153783 (more recently transferred to the Royal Air Force as F-4J(UK) ZE352) and for a shorter time by a second Phantom. The paint scheme on the Tomcat was less popular with the Top Brass and was quickly removed [*Jeff Puzzullo*]

Photographed in February 1975 at NAS Patuxent River, Maryland, this high-visibility F-14A was in fact the seventeenth example delivered to the Navy in mid-November 1972. Mounted on the centreline stores station is a Mk82 500 lb bomb, this aircraft being tasked to test the Tomcat's attack capability. Sitting snugly in the back seat is a fully-clothed RIO dummy which answers to the name of 'Clyde' [*Lionel N Paul*]

Inset Grumman F-14A Tomcat 158631 with its side number from the 'last three' of the serial is one of a number of F-14s at the Strike Test Directorate, NATC Patuxent River, Maryland [*Lionel N Paul*]

Inset Wearing a tiny 'Anytime Baby' sticker atop its fin, and the rather bland Service Test Division's stylized 'S' alongside the rudder, this F-14A was in fact the last of eight 'Block' 60 Tomcats delivered to the Navy in 1973. Seen on the ramp at Oceana in April 1973, 158619 was lost four years later at Pax River when the aircraft entered a deadly flat spin during stall trials of the Pratt & Whitney TF30-P-414. Unfortunately one of the crew failed to bang out of the stricken Tomcat and was killed [*Allan Van Dam*]

An unpublished view of one Soviet-designed aircraft type which has fallen prey to the mighty Tomcat. The MiG-23, shown here with a hefty load of missiles, is decidedly second-best in the air combat arena. In a fluke engagement over international waters, VF-32 'Swordsmen' Tomcats shot down two Libyan MiG-23s on 4 January 1989. Now approaching the twentieth anniversary of its entry into squadron service, the Tomcat itself is an older design than such Soviet types as the MiG-29 and MiG-31 and is increasingly taxed in its principal duty of guarding the Fleet from bombers and cruise missiles – but it would be a big mistake to write the Tomcat off at any point in the remainder of the century [*Bill Henry*]

At one time the US Marine Corps expected to receive some F-14 Tomcats to replace its F-4 Phantoms. In the end, the Marines did not become Tomcat users (nor did the US Air Force, which had pondered an interceptor version) and their Phantoms remained in use longer than originally planned. Typical of the final Phantoms in use among naval units is F-4S 155900, coded MG-12, of the 'Hell's Angels' of VMFA-321, the reserve fighter squadron at Andrews AFB, Maryland. The squadron was some distance from home when this take-off was recorded at the London Ontario Airshow on 4 June 1989 [*Barry Roop*]

Above General Dynamics F-111B 151974, the Navy's part of the famous McNamara TFX fighter project, shows why it has a turning radius suitable for carrier operations. It seemed a good idea early in the Kennedy administration, developing a fighter which both the Navy and Air Force could use, but the Navy didn't agree and the F-111B never became part of any carrier air wing. What *did* happen was that the AGM-54A Phoenix missile, developed in connection with the TFX/F-111B programme, was well on its way toward reaching final design when the Grumman F-14 Tomcat came along a decade later [*via Authors*]

Right An early Tomcat from an unusual angle. This highly colourful aircraft had just been delivered to VF-124 'Gunfighters' when this photo was taken at Miramar on 23 October 1976. The 'Gunfighters' have the distinction of being associated with the F-14 longer than any other squadron, the first Grumman fighters appearing on VF-124's books in October 1972 [*Mike Henning*]

This page and overleaf 157986 is a unique Tomcat. As the sole testbed for the F-14B model, it was powered by twin Pratt & Whitney F401-PW-400 engines. The F-14B was not ordered into production but this airframe remained at the Grumman plant to become the prototype F-14A + (Plus) with General Electric F110-GE-400 engines. The latter powerplant will also be employed by the forthcoming F-14D [*Grumman*]